The Best Juicing Cookbook

Get the Best Juice Recipes for Any Occasion

BY: Ivy Hope

Copyright © 2021 by Ivy Hope

Copyright/License Page

Please don't reproduce this book. It means you are not allowed to make any type of copy (print or electronic), sell, publish, disseminate or distribute. Only people who have written permission from the author are allowed to do so.

This book is written by the author taking all precautions that the content is true and helpful. However, the reader needs to be careful about his/her action. If anything happens due to the reader's actions the author won't be taken as responsible.

Table of Contents

Introduction 7

Chapter 1: Breakfast Juices 9

    Peach Pineapple Morning Juice 10

    Apple Beet Juice 12

    Morning Melon Magic 14

    Double Applenade 16

    Orange Beet Juice 18

    Merry Melon 20

    Kokomo Coconut 22

    Apple Cranberry Magic 24

    Grape Fizzy 26

    Berry Blast 28

Chapter 2: Juices on the Move 30

    Melon Citrus Juice 31

    Summer Lemon Splash 33

    Icy Island Juice 35

Apple Juice 37

Smart-N-Tart Lemonade 39

Blazing Blackberries 40

Garden Goose Juice 42

Peach Punch 44

Celery Soda 46

Cherries Plum Delight 48

Chapter 3: Drinks for Dessert 50

Lemon Sparkleberry 51

Dazzling Berry 53

Kiwi Apple Juice 55

Green Party Punch 57

Super Melon Man 59

Banana Juice 61

Pink Melon Drink 63

Orange Lemonade 65

Cherry Melon 67

Blue-nana Juice 69

Chapter 4: Fruit and Vegetable Combos 71

    Sweet Potato and Apple Juice 72

    Berry Powerful Juice 74

    Asian-inspired Citrus Cabbage Blend 76

    Spicy Apple Lemonade 78

    Apple Squash Dessert Juice 80

    Spicy Orange Pineapple Juice 82

    Ginger Pear Juice 84

    Nutritious Peach Juice 86

    Red Summer Cooler 88

    Vegetable Citrus Medley 90

Chapter 5: Green Juices 92

    Green Mix Juice 93

    Kale Cucumber Green Juice 95

    Celery Apple Mix Juice 97

    Lettuce Apple Green Juice 99

    Grapefruit Lettuce Green Juice 101

    Kiwi Grape Green Juice 103

Swiss Chard Green Juice 105

Green Pineapple Juice 107

Blackberry Mint Green Juice 109

Carrot Broccoli Juice 111

Conclusion 113

About the Author 114

Author's Afterthoughts 115

Introduction

Juicing is the process of extracting fluid from fruits and vegetables, and it's the second simplest thing you can do with those ingredients after eating them raw. After all, all the nutrients haven't been released when you eat them in their raw state.

Juices are a great way to incorporate more fruits and vegetables into your diet. They can help you get essential vitamins and minerals, especially if your diet is not very meat-oriented.

Juices can provide you with an immediate energy boost. Some nutritionists claim that juicing is not ideal for those who are looking to lose weight, but the truth is that if you consume your juices at mealtime, they can help you lose as much weight as regular foods.

A simple way to juice vegetables is to make a so-called "Mason Jar Juice." This requires only a few basic ingredients, and it's very easy to follow. You basically place your vegetable or fruit in the mason jar, put the lid on, and press down. The result is a highly nutritious liquid that can be drunk directly.

Juices have become trendy, just like juicing herbs or making juices from fruits and vegetables that are already ripe. Juicing has become more of a hobby than a necessity, and that's why we have come up with this juicing recipe book.

There are plenty of juice recipes here that can help you lose weight, as well as other healthy habits.

This is a juicing recipe book that will serve as an introduction to the readers, as well as being an on-the-go guide for those of you who want to spend less time in the kitchen and more time enjoying your juices.

Chapter 1: Breakfast Juices

Peach Pineapple Morning Juice

Nothing starts your engines better in the morning than a glass full of manganese. This trace mineral, contained in high doses in pineapple, is an essential coenzyme for energy production.

Prep time: 4 minutes

Servings: 4

Ingredients:

- 1½ cups fresh pineapple
- 1 peach, pitted
- 3 tablespoons water

Instructions:

1. Place both the pineapple and the peach in a juicer and run through the juicer.

2. Mix thoroughly together. If the juice is too thick, dilute with the water a tablespoon at a time until it's the consistency your kids like.

Apple Beet Juice

Drinking this beet juice gives you energy and a variety of nutrients. When you drink this juice, glucose from the fruit is easily absorbed into cells to become a primary energy source.

Prep time: 4 minutes

Servings: 2

Ingredients:

- 1 beet, peeled and greens removed
- 2 red apples, cored

Instructions:

1. Place beet and apples into a juicer and turn on.

2. Collect the juice in a pitcher and stir to combine.

Morning Melon Magic

This fresh melon juice is an ideal way to kick start your day after an overnight fast. The melon and cucumber mixture makes this juice very refreshing and very satisfying!

Prep time: 5 minutes

Servings: 1

Ingredients:

- 1 cucumber, peeled
- ½ honeydew melon

Instructions:

1. Peel the cucumber and then juice it.

2. Scoop the flesh out of the melon and then juice the flesh only.

3. Stir the juices together thoroughly till dissolved in each other.

Double Applenade

With antioxidants and vitamin C, this "double the apple juice" juice has the ability to keep you healthy. Not only will it boost your immune systems, but it will also increase heart health and help keep your arteries clean.

Prep time: 5 minutes

Servings: 2

Ingredients:

- 2 red apples, cored
- 1 apple, cored
- ¼ lemon, cut in half

Instructions:

1. Juice both types of apples and then the lemon, including the rind.

2. Collect into a pitcher and stir before serving.

Orange Beet Juice

A daily dose of beet juice can help kids retain their memory by increasing blood flow to the brain. Serve this juice up in the morning of a big test and give you an extra advantage.

Prep time: 4 minutes

Servings: 2

Ingredients:

- 2 oranges, peeled
- 1 beet, peeled and greens removed

Instructions:

1. Push orange and beet through a juicer as it's running.

2. Collect the juice into one container and stir.

Merry Melon

You can smell a cantaloupe even before cutting into it. I guarantee you that everyone, especially your kids, will love this drink!

Prep time: 5 minutes

Servings: 3

Ingredients:

- ½ cantaloupe, rind removed
- 1 cup strawberries

Instructions:

1. Juice the strawberries and cantaloupe with a juicer.

2. Stir and then serve.

Kokomo Coconut

This juice has all the makings to start a breezy summer day off just right—or to bring a little island paradise to a rainy fall day.

Prep time: 5 minutes

Servings: 3

Ingredients:

- 1 papaya, seeded
- ½ lime, peeled
- 1 cup unsweetened coconut milk

Instructions:

1. Juice the papaya and lime into a single pitcher.

2. Stir in the coconut milk until well combined.

Apple Cranberry Magic

Turn a mundane cereal breakfast into a fancy feast just by serving some homemade cranberry juice with your meal. Adding fruit juice helps you to get a balanced meal and fill them up until lunch.

Prep time: 4 minutes

Servings: 2

Ingredients:

- 1¼ cups cranberries
- 2 red apples, cored

Instructions:

1. Juice the cranberries and apples into a single pitcher.

2. Stir the juices together until well combined.

Grape Fizzy

This grape juice has everything you love about grape juice, without the stains. When the kids inevitably spill their juice, you will not need to run to the rescue right away!

Prep time: 4 minutes

Servings: 2

Ingredients:

- 1½ cups green seedless grapes
- 2 limes, peeled

Instructions:

1. Put the grapes, then the lime, through the spout of a juicer and juice.

2. Combine both juices and stir thoroughly.

Berry Blast

With the shelf life of strawberries being so incredibly short, you'll save money by juicing your uneaten strawberries before they have a chance to go bad.

Prep time: 5 minutes

Servings: 4

Ingredients:

- ½ average cantaloupe
- 2 cups strawberries

Instructions:

1. Juice cantaloupe and strawberries together.

2. Stir thoroughly until the juice is well blended.

Chapter 2: Juices on the Move

Melon Citrus Juice

Want to quench your thirst? This juice will refresh and quench your thirst, leaving you fully hydrated.

Prep time: 4 minutes

Servings: 2

Ingredients:

- 2 cups watermelon, rind removed
- 2 oranges, peeled

Instructions:

1. Peel the oranges and juice them and the watermelon in a juicer.

2. Stir and serve.

Summer Lemon Splash

This lemon-cucumber water is perfect for taking to the swimming pool during the hot days of summer. It's refreshing and light and great for hydrating on the go.

Prep time: 5 minutes

Servings: 4

Ingredients:

- 1 lemon, peeled
- 2 cucumbers, peeled
- 1 cup ice-cold water

Instructions:

1. Juice lemon and cucumber.

2. Stir in ice cold water until it is all combined.

Icy Island Juice

If you want to have an island's taste at the comfort of your home, this recipe is the perfect solution. It will give you that vacation feeling that is very refreshing.

Prep time: 4 minutes

Servings: 3

Ingredients:

- 1 cup pineapple, peeled
- 7 large strawberries, hull intact
- ½ papaya, seeds removed

Instructions:

1. One at a time, juice strawberries, papaya, and pineapple with a juicer and collect in a container.

2. Serve immediately.

Apple Juice

Next time your family heads out for a hike in the mountains, fill empty water bottles with this apple-grape juice. Partially freeze it to save for the middle of the hike when everyone is extra hot and thirsty. It will be refreshing and give them the boost they need to finish the hike!

Prep time: 4 minutes

Servings: 2

Ingredients:

- 2 red apples, cored
- 1 cup green seedless grapes

Instructions:

1. Push the apples and the grapes through the input spout of a juicer, and juice.

2. Collect the juice in a single container or bottle, and stir to combined both juices.

Smart-N-Tart Lemonade

This drink is ideal for child athletes to keep them hydrated as it is a sugar-free sports drink. It is way much better than lemon-flavored sports drinks.

Prep time: 4 minutes

Servings: 2

Ingredients:

- 2 cucumbers, peeled
- 1 lemon, peeled

Instructions:

1. Juice the lemon and cucumbers using a juicer.

2. Stir and serve in glasses.

Blazing Blackberries

If you are undecided on what drink to leave for your kids when you are not around, this is the best option. This recipe is a superfood that will keep them energized for long.

Prep time: 4 minutes

Servings: 2

Ingredients:

- 2 pints blackberries
- ½ lemon, peeled
- 1 banana

Instructions:

1. Juice banana, lemon, and blackberries with a juicer.

2. Stir and serve.

Garden Goose Juice

Forget about spending the next day trying to use up your zucchini for bread. Spend 5 minutes and juice it instead. Adding some apples to this zucchini juice brings out the sweetness of the fall flavors.

Prep time: 5 minutes

Servings: 2

Ingredients:

- 1 green zucchini
- 3 carrots, peeled
- 2 red apples, cored

Instructions:

1. First, juice the carrots, apples, and zucchini into a large glass.

2. Next, stir the juices together till they are combined.

Peach Punch

Pick up a whole box of peaches so you'll have enough fruit to eat some fresh as well as to make this delicious peach strawberry juice. You will enjoy the fruity taste.

Prep time: 4 minutes

Servings: 3

Ingredients:

- 7 large strawberries, hulls intact
- 1 large peach, pitted

Instructions:

1. Take peach and strawberries, push through the spout of a juicer, and juice.

2. Collect juice into a single container, and stir till juices are well blended.

Celery Soda

When the kids are asking for apple juice, don't be afraid to add a little celery to their cup. As an excellent source of vitamins C and K, celery boosts the nutritional value of plain apple juice.

Prep time: 4 minutes

Servings: 3

Ingredients:

- 2 celery stalks
- 1 apple, cored

Instructions:

1. Juice the apple and then the celery.

2. Collect in a single container, and stir before serving.

Cherries Plum Delight

This drink will lift blood sugar to a level that will put smiles on your kids' faces.

Prep time: 4 minutes

Servings: 2

Ingredients:

- 1½ cups cherries, pitted
- 2 black plums, pitted

Instructions:

1. Push cherries and plums through the spout of a juicer, and turn on.

2. Continue to push the fruit through until it has all been juiced.

3. Collect the juice in a single container, and stir before serving.

Chapter 3: Drinks for Dessert

Lemon Sparkleberry

This lemon-lime drink has all the party pizzazz of the real thing without sugar. Let's try it!

Prep time: 5 minutes

Servings: 4

Ingredients:

- 3 lemons, cut into pieces (including the rind)
- 3 limes, cut into pieces (including the rind)
- 4 cups sparkling water

Instructions:

1. Juice the limes and lemons with a juicer.

2. Serve into 4 glasses and top each glass with a cup of sparkling water.

Dazzling Berry

Turn simple berry juice into a party drink with a dollop of whipped topping and sprinkles. Give kids their own cups to decorate and keep for the refills they'll be asking for.

Prep time: 4 minutes

Servings: 2

Ingredients:

- 2 cups raspberries
- 2 cups strawberries, hulls intact

Instructions:

Juice the strawberries and the raspberries together.

Combine the juice, and stir until well mixed.

Kiwi Apple Juice

High in fiber, this dessert drink is a great follow-up to party fare that may be less than healthy. Get that party cake moving quickly through digestion by following it with this juice, and you won't feel sick after the big day.

Prep time: 4 minutes

Servings: 2

Ingredients:

- 2 red apples, cut in half
- 3 kiwis, peeled

Instructions:

1. Push apples and kiwis into a juicer, and run through until completely juiced.

2. Collect juice from both fruits through collection spout, and stir.

Green Party Punch

No drink served at a party can stand a nutritional chance against this vitamin-packed party punch. Full of vegetable greens and herbs, this drink will have kids talking about it long after the balloons have popped.

Prep time: 5 minutes

Servings: 4

Ingredients:

- 1 bunch spinach
- 1 cucumber, peeled
- ½ bunch celery, including the leaves
- 1 bunch parsley
- ½" piece fresh ginger root
- 2 green apples, cored
- ½ lime, peeled
- ½ lemon, peeled

Instructions:

1. Juice each fruit or vegetable one at a time, collecting juice extract into one large bowl.

2. Stir juices together to combine.

Super Melon Man

This juice is a delicious blend of watermelon, cantaloupe, and orange. It is rich in folate, vitamin K, and magnesium, all of which support healthy bones.

Prep time: 4 minutes

Servings: 3

Ingredients:

- 1 cup watermelon, rind removed
- 1 cup cantaloupe, rind removed
- 1 orange, peeled

Instructions:

1. Juice all three fruits until they have all been processed.

2. Collect all juice into one container, and stir to mix fruit juices together.

Banana Juice

Kick back for a family movie night with this juice, some popcorn, and some candied nuts. The apples and blackberries are sweet and yummy, and the lemon delivers some thirst-quenching action.

Prep time: 4 minutes

Servings: 3

Ingredients:

- 2 apples
- 2 cups blackberries
- 1 lemon, peeled
- 1 banana, peeled

Instructions:

1. Juice the apples, blackberries, lemon, and then the banana in a single pitcher.

2. Stir together until the juices are well blended.

Pink Melon Drink

The ingredients were chosen not only for their taste but also for their ability to promote good health. This drink will improve the appearance of the skin, and cinnamon boosts energy and may accelerate weight loss.

Prep time: 4 minutes

Servings: 2

Ingredients:

- 1 cup watermelon, rind removed
- 1 lime, peeled

Instructions:

1. First, juice the watermelon, then the lime.

2. Collect juices from both fruits into one cup, and stir before serving.

Orange Lemonade

Simple and sweet, this orange-and-lemon drink only needs two ingredients. Serve this juice for a refreshing mid-afternoon pick-me-up and it is sure to wake up tired tots.

Prep time: 4 minutes

Servings: 2

Ingredients:

- 3 oranges, peeled
- 1 lemon, peeled

Instructions:

1. Juice the orange and the lemon together.

2. Stir before serving.

Cherry Melon

Scoop melon balls out of a watermelon and cantaloupe. Then let the melon balls float on top of this juice, served in a punch bowl. Cherries are a superfood because they have loads of antioxidants whether you eat them fresh, juiced, dried, or frozen!

Prep time: 4 minutes

Servings: 2

Ingredients:

- 1 cup watermelon, rind removed
- 1 cup cherries, pitted
- ½ lime, peeled

Instructions:

1. Juice the watermelon, cherries, and lime into one container.

2. Stir juices together, and top with melon balls.

Blue-nana Juice

The rich color in this blueberry juice gives away the fact that it is packed with the dark blue phytonutrient, anthocyanin. Although you would assume a sweet drink like this would raise blood sugar, anthocyanins have the opposite effect and can actually reduce the risk of diabetes.

Prep time: 4 minutes

Servings: 3

Ingredients:

- 2 cups blueberries
- 1 banana, peeled

Instructions:

1. Place blueberries and banana in a juicer, and turn the juicer on.

2. Collect the juice in one cup, and stir before serving.

Chapter 4: Fruit and Vegetable Combos

Sweet Potato and Apple Juice

The mild flavor of the sweet potatoes combines well with the mellow carrots, peppers, and apples in this recipe, while tangerines offer a little bit of sweetness. In addition to a great taste, this juice provides plenty of vitamin A and folate.

Prep time: 5 minutes

Servings: 3

Ingredients:

- 3 sweet tangerines
- 2 sweet golden apples
- 2 large carrots
- 1 medium raw sweet potato
- 1 medium sweet red pepper

Instructions:

1. Peel the tangerines and remove any seeds. Wash all the other ingredients thoroughly.

2. Cut off the stem ends of the carrots and pepper, removing the seeds and ribs from the pepper.

3. Remove the stem and seeds from the apples and peel the sweet potato, cutting it into large cubes.

4. Process all of the ingredients in a powerful blender or juicer, saving one tangerine for last.

Berry Powerful Juice

Grapes and berries make a flavorful juice that supplies plenty of anti-oxidant compounds, but they can't provide all the nutrition your body needs. That's why combining them with fresh dark leafy greens such as kale or spinach is such a smart idea.

Prep time: 5 minutes

Servings: 4

Ingredients:

- 2 cups blueberries or raspberries
- 2 cups red or Concord grapes
- 1 cup fresh kale
- 1 cup fresh spinach

Instructions:

1. Wash the fruit thoroughly. Remove the grapes from their stems and discard the stems.

2. Remove any wilted or yellow leaves from the kale and spinach. Process all the fruit and vegetables in a juicer or powerful blender, adding water if necessary.

3. Chill and drink along with a light snack.

4. Add 2 tablespoons of your favorite protein powder for a meal replacement drink.

Asian-inspired Citrus Cabbage Blend

Fresh cabbage has a crisp texture and zesty flavor that makes it the star of some unusual salads as well as this delightful juice. The combination of tropical citrus, Asian pears and other Chinese ingredients will be your new favorite for sure!

Prep time: 5 minutes

Servings: 3

Ingredients:

- 1 small head bok choy, napa or green cabbage
- 3 medium carrots
- 2 tart green apples
- 2 Persian limes
- 1 lemon
- 1 Asian pear
- 1 thumb-length of ginger

Instructions:

1. Peel the lemon and limes.

2. Wash the cabbage, carrots, pear and apples thoroughly.

3. Remove the seeds and stems from the apples and pear. Cut off the stem end from the carrots and chop the cabbage into manageable chunks.

4. Process all the ingredients in a juicer or blender, starting and finishing with an apple.

5. Pour over ice and serve.

Spicy Apple Lemonade

This flavorful fruit juice includes a sweet yellow pepper to boost its nutritional value. You'll enjoy the cleansing effects of this beverage, as well as its mild, pleasant flavor. To increase tartness, simply add another lemon to the mix.

Prep time: 5 minutes

Servings: 2

Ingredients:

- 3 large sweet apples, such as Fuji
- 1 lemon
- 1 sweet yellow bell pepper
- 1 tablespoon ginger

Instructions:

1. Peel the lemon and remove any seeds.

2. Wash the pepper and apples thoroughly to get rid of dirt and chemical residues. Seed all the apples and remove the seeds, stem and interior ribs from the pepper.

3. Add all ingredients to a powerful blender or a juicer with a large screen and process until smooth. Drink chilled.

Apple Squash Dessert Juice

This recipe offers some of the same flavors you'll find in a good, natural apple pie, including the spicy zip of cinnamon. That's why it's such a great choice for anyone who craves dessert but prefers a healthy option.

Prep time: 5 minutes

Servings: 2

Ingredients:

- 1 medium butternut squash (about 1 ½ pounds)
- 4 medium sweet apples
- 1 teaspoon ground cinnamon

Instructions:

1. Wash the apples and squash to remove dirt and chemical residues.

2. Slice the squash in half, remove the seeds, and cut the flesh into large cubes.

3. De-seed the apple and remove its stem. Run the apple and the squash cubes through your blender or juicer, adding water as necessary.

4. Stir in the cinnamon and garnish with a cinnamon stick if desired.

Spicy Orange Pineapple Juice

Orange and pineapple are a classic combination, but on their own, they can be overpowering. That's why this hearty juice includes lime, carrots, and chili. The more complex flavor is sure to be a winner at your table.

Prep time: 5 minutes

Servings: 2

Ingredients:

- 2 sweet juicing oranges, such as Valencia or Moro
- 1 medium carrot
- 1 cup chopped pineapple
- 1 lime
- 1 small red pepper

Instructions:

1. Peel the citrus fruits and remove any seeds. Wash the carrot and remove any core or peel from the pineapple.

2. Combine all ingredients in a blender or juicer with enough water to produce a smooth, drinkable consistency.

Ginger Pear Juice

Pears and ginger are another classic combination that's found in crisps, ciders, and a range of other foods. Pears provide plenty of fiber, while ginger helps promote healthy digestion, making this an excellent juice for anyone who has recently overindulged.

Prep time: 5 minutes

Servings: 2

Instructions:

- 1 medium pear
- 1 stalk celery
- 1 tablespoon fresh ginger

Ingredients:

1. Wash all ingredients and remove the stem and seeds from the pear.

2. Combine the fruit and ginger in a blender or juicer, processing until smooth.

Nutritious Peach Juice

This flavorful juice includes strong-tasting fruits that effectively cover the taste of nutrition-packed greens like broccoli and spinach. While the color of this juice recipe might be a little surprising, the flavor and nutrient profile simply can't be beaten.

Prep time: 5 minutes

Servings: 2

Instructions:

- 3 ripe peaches
- 1 tart apple
- 2 stalks broccoli
- 1 cup spinach leaves

Ingredients:

1. Wash all fruits and vegetables thoroughly. Remove the tough ends of the broccoli, the pits from the peaches, and the seeds from the apples.

2. Place all ingredients in a blender or juicer and process until smooth. The result may be slightly brownish in color, but the flavor will be all fruit.

Red Summer Cooler

This interesting juice fast recipe combines the classic pairing of tomatoes and basil with sweet red strawberries. The best berries are organic, local, and in season, but if these aren't available, you can choose fragrant berries and wash them well.

Prep Time: 5 minutes

Servings: 2

Instructions:

- 1 pound ripe red tomatoes
- ½ pound whole strawberries
- 5 leaves sweet basil

Ingredients:

1. Hull the strawberries and tomatoes, discarding the leaves.

2. If necessary, cut the tomatoes into pieces your juicer is able to handle.

3. Process the fruit and basil leaves together to produce a strikingly red, flavorful beverage. Serve over ice.

Vegetable Citrus Medley

This drink is rich in a variety of vitamins, minerals, and phytonutrients. While it uses vegetables more usually associated with soups and stews, that shouldn't put you off. The result is a complex beverage with an unusual color and plenty of health-promoting properties.

Prep Time: 4 minutes

Servings: 2

Ingredients:

- 2 large juicing oranges
- 1 medium carrot
- 1 small lemon
- 1 stalk celery
- ½ cup raw red beets
- ½ cup spinach leaves

Instructions:

1. Peel the citrus fruits and remove any seeds. Wash the greens and other vegetables thoroughly.

2. Process the lemon and oranges first, followed by the leafy greens.

3. Use the celery and carrots to push any leftover material through your juicer. Serve over ice with ginger if desired.

Chapter 5: Green Juices

Green Mix Juice

This green juice is chock-full of antioxidants and other nutrients that benefit your brain, eyes, hair, muscles, and nails. Let's try it!

Prep Time: 5 minutes

Servings: 2

Ingredients:

- 1 celery stalk with leaves
- 1 green apple
- 2 large kale leaves
- 1 cucumber
- ½-inch piece of ginger
- 1 handful spinach leaves
- 1 handful mint leaves
- Juice of 2 limes
- 2 Tbsp stevia or raw sugar
- ¼ Tbsp salt flakes
- 2 cup of cold water
- 1 Tbsp spirulina powder

Instructions:

1. Prepare all ingredients — cut, wash, peel and deseed, when possible.

2. Put them into a juicer and process until smooth.

3. Add enough water and sugar to get the desired sweetness and consistency (optional).

4. Pour into a glass (optionally through a sieve), serve chilled.

Kale Cucumber Green Juice

This is the perfect green juice if you have a demanding work schedule. Take it with you to the office and sip while working. This juice will keep your body hydrated and your mind clear.

Prep Time: 5 minutes

Servings: 2

Ingredients:

- 1 cucumber
- 4 celery stalks
- 2 apples
- 6-8 kale leaves
- ½ lemon
- 1 Tbsp ginger

Instructions:

1. Prepare all ingredients — cut, wash, peel and deseed, when possible.

2. Put them into a juicer and process until smooth.

3. Add enough water and sugar to get the desired sweetness and consistency (optional).

4. Pour into a glass (optionally through a sieve), serve chilled.

Celery Apple Mix Juice

This juice is so healthy and energizing. The red apple adds wonderful color to the juice, and the fruit is great for your heart and your skin.

Prep Time: 5 minutes

Servings: 2

Ingredients:

- 1 bunch celery
- 1 medium cucumber
- 1 green pepper
- 1 red apple
- 1 orange
- ½ of lemon

Instructions:

1. Prepare all ingredients — cut, wash, peel and deseed, when possible.

2. Put them into a juicer and process until smooth.

3. Add enough water and sugar to get the desired sweetness and consistency (optional).

4. Pour into a glass (optionally through a sieve), serve chilled.

Lettuce Apple Green Juice

This recipe will improve your digestion as it contains a soluble fiber called pectin that comes from apples. The lettuce, on the other hand, have antioxidants responsible for the protection of the stomach lining.

Prep Time: 5 minutes

Servings: 2

Ingredients:

- 2 red lettuce heads
- 2 medium pears or apple
- ½ lemon
- 1 medium cucumber

Instructions:

1. Prepare all ingredients — cut, wash, peel and deseed, when possible.

2. Put them into a juicer and process until smooth.

3. Add enough water and sugar to get the desired sweetness and consistency (optional).

4. Pour into a glass (optionally through a sieve), serve chilled.

Grapefruit Lettuce Green Juice

Grapefruit is often included in weight loss diets because of its ability to help you feel full and burn fat. In green juice, grapefruit becomes an essential part of a healthy morning routine.

Servings: 2

Prep Time: 5 minutes

Ingredients:

- 1 pink grapefruit
- 1 head romaine lettuce
- 2 oranges
- 1 bunch mint

Directions:

1. Prepare all ingredients — cut, wash, peel and deseed, when possible.

2. Put them into a juicer and process until smooth.

3. Add enough water and sugar to get the desired sweetness and consistency (optional).

4. Pour into a glass (optionally through a sieve), serve chilled.

Kiwi Grape Green Juice

The bright green color of this juice will delight your eyes as much as its sweet yet slightly tart flavor appeals to your taste buds. Kiwis are a popular fruit known for their ability to firm skin, control excess sebum production, lighten dark circles, and prevent premature gray hair.

Servings: 1 - 2

Prep Time: 5 minutes

Ingredients:

- 2½ field cucumbers
- 1 cup green grapes
- ½ cup spinach
- 2 small kiwis
- 1–2 cup water

Instructions:

1. Prepare all ingredients — cut, wash, peel and deseed, when possible.

2. Put them into a juicer and process until smooth.

3. Add enough water and sugar to get the desired sweetness and consistency (optional).

4. Pour into a glass (optionally through a sieve), serve chilled.

Swiss Chard Green Juice

This straightforward recipe brims with good ingredients that will make your skin feel hydrated and supple.

Servings: 2

Prep Time: 5 minutes

Ingredients:

- 1 bunch Swiss chard
- 2 large lemons
- 1 medium pear
- 1 medium cucumber
- 2 green apples
- 1 Tbsp raw, unfiltered honey per serving

Directions:

1. Prepare all ingredients — cut, wash, peel and deseed, when possible.

2. Put them into a juicer and process until smooth.

3. Add enough water and sugar to get the desired sweetness and consistency (optional).

4. Pour into a glass (optionally through a sieve), stir in honey, serve chilled.

Green Pineapple Juice

Pineapple is bright and tastes fresh. It also contains the enzyme bromelain, which relieves inflammation and helps with poor digestion. Choose this juice for a dynamic weight loss and detoxification combo.

Servings: 2

Prep Time: 5 minutes

Ingredients:

- 1 cucumber
- 1 romaine lettuce heart
- 3 celery sticks
- 4 cup pineapple
- 1-inch piece of ginger
- ½ cup coconut water

Instructions:

1. Prepare all ingredients — cut, wash, peel and deseed, when possible.

2. Put them into a juicer and process until smooth.

3. Add enough water and sugar to get the desired sweetness and consistency (optional).

4. Pour into a glass (optionally through a sieve), serve chilled.

Blackberry Mint Green Juice

The mint stimulates your mind, the kale detoxifies your body, and the blackberries keep you looking and feeling vibrant.

Servings: 2

Prep Time: 5 minutes

Ingredients:

- 1 cup blackberries
- 1 lemon
- 1 small cucumber
- 1 handful of watercress
- 1 cup broccoli
- 2 small green apples
- 2 stalks kale
- ½ a fennel bulb with greens
- 4 sprigs mint

Instructions:

1. Prepare all ingredients — cut, wash, peel and deseed, when possible.

2. Put them into a juicer and process until smooth.

3. Add enough water and sugar to get the desired sweetness and consistency (optional).

4. Pour into a glass (optionally through a sieve), and top with springs of mint.

Carrot Broccoli Juice

Broccoli deserves an award for its supporting role in this juice. This juice has a surprisingly mellow flavor, yet it has powerful effects. It helps reduce inflammation, control blood sugar, and protect against cancer.

Servings: 2

Prep Time: 5 minutes

Ingredients:

- 1 bunch celery
- 1 medium carrot
- 1 whole broccoli
- 1 Fuji apple
- ½ lemon

Instructions:

1. Prepare all ingredients — cut, wash, peel and deseed, when possible.

2. Put them into a juicer and process until smooth.

3. Add enough water and sugar to get the desired sweetness and consistency (optional).

4. Pour into a glass (optionally through a sieve), serve chilled.

Conclusion

Thank you for getting to the end of this book. I hope you have had lots of fun preparing the recipes in this book.

Happy juicing!

About the Author

Ivy's mission is to share her recipes with the world. Even though she is not a professional cook she has always had that flair toward cooking. Her hands create magic. She can make even the simplest recipe tastes superb. Everyone who has tried her food has astounding their compliments was what made her think about writing recipes.She wanted everyone to have a taste of her creations aside from close family and friends. So, deciding to write recipes was her winning decision. She isn't interested in popularity, but how many people have her recipes reached and touched people. Each recipe in her cookbooks is special and has a special meaning in her life. This means that each recipe is created with attention and love. Every ingredient carefully picked, every combination tried and tested.Her mission started on her birthday about 9 years ago, when her guests couldn't stop prizing the food on the table. The next thing she did was organizing an event where chefs from restaurants were tasting her recipes. This event gave her the courage to start spreading her recipes.She has written many cookbooks and she is still working on more. There is no end in the art of cooking; all you need is inspiration, love, and dedication.

Author's Afterthoughts

THANK YOU

I am thankful for downloading this book and taking the time to read it. I know that you have learned a lot and you had a great time reading it. Writing books is the best way to share the skills I have with your and the best tips too.

I know that there are many books and choosing my book is amazing. I am thankful that you stopped and took time to decide. You made a great decision and I am sure that you enjoyed it.

I will be even happier if you provide honest feedback about my book. Feedbacks helped by growing and they still do. They help me to choose better content and new ideas. So, maybe your feedback can trigger an idea for my next book.

Thank you again

Sincerely

Ivy Hope

Printed in Great Britain
by Amazon